MODERN KID PRESS

W9-BJC-668

# SIGHT WORDS &
# SPELLING
## —WORKBOOK—

for kids
AGES
6-8

# Email us at

## modernkidpress@gmail.com

# to get free extras!

---

Just title the email "Spelling"
And we will send some extra
surprises your way!

We finally joined Instagram!
Come check us out at

## @modernkidpress!

This book belongs to

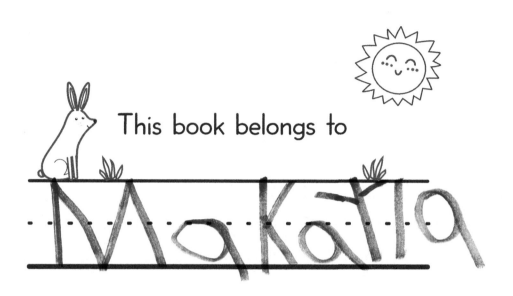

Makayla

# Hey there!

Let's spell together! When you work through the following 22 spelling units:

**1) Look at the spelling word**

**2) Say the word aloud**

**3) Write the word**

Check your spelling of each word after you have finished.

Don't forget to have fun!

# UNIT 1

 Trace each word, then write it twice more in the space provided.

> them

> to

> and

> you

> on

> it

> said

> up

> look

> see

✏️ Write each of your spelling words in the stars below.

Put the following words into their correct shape boxes.

**WORD BANK:**

look    and    you

 Draw a line to connect the matching words.

| | |
|---|---|
| look | it |
| you | up |
| up | you |
| it | look |
| on | on |

Circle the correct spelling in each row.

| | | | |
|---|---|---|---|
| thi | the | tee | thi |
| sid | sed | said | ced |
| amd | ann | and | anb |
| see | se | cee | sei |
| yiu | yuo | yu | you |
| onn | on | un | ono |

you            look

them            see

 Use the words to the left to fill in the spaces and complete the story!

Can _____ see the stars?

I do not see _____.

Just _____ up.

I _____ them!

# UNIT 2

 Trace each word, then write it twice more in the space provided.

> is

> go

> we

> little

> down

> but

> can

> for

> not

> one

Write each of your spelling words in the gems below.

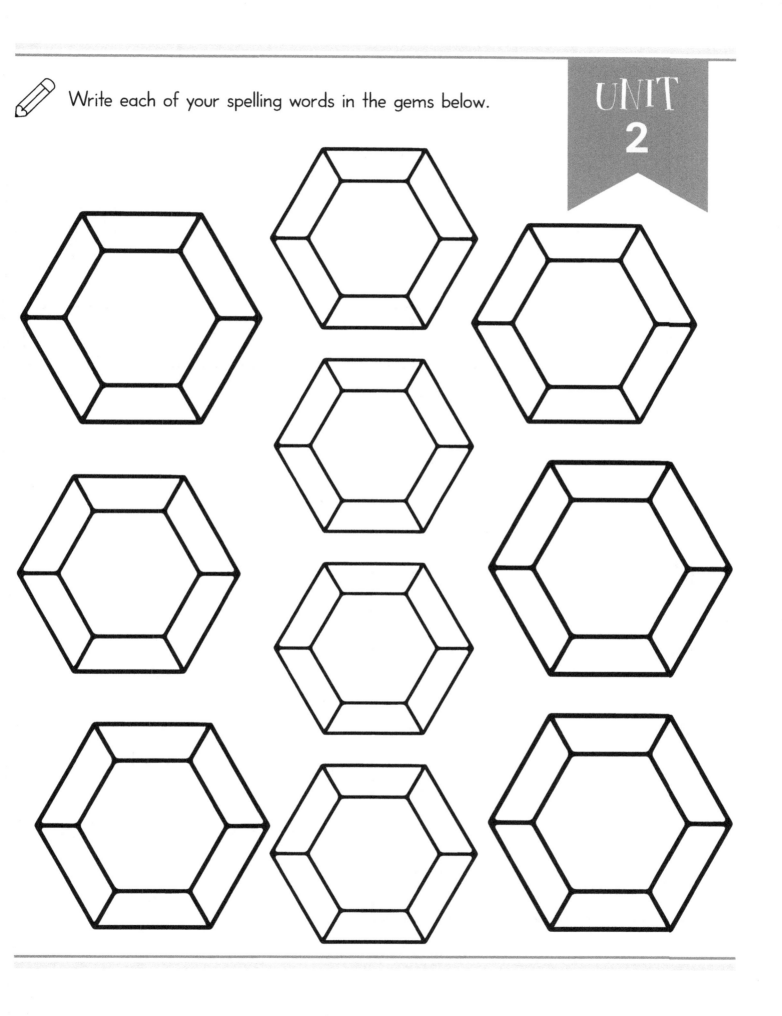

Put the following words into their correct shape boxes.

**WORD BANK:**

go     down     one

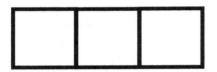

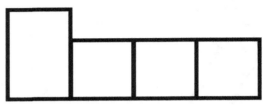

---

 Draw a line to connect the matching words.

| little | but |
| is | can |
| we | little |
| can | is |
| but | we |

 Circle the correct spelling in each row.

| can | cen | cann | cna |
| litle | littlle | little | lettle |
| one | oin | oine | oen |
| buw | but | bugt | bat |
| down | doun | doww | donn |
| wui | wee | wie | we |

1) Fill in the missing letter for each word.
2) Read each word aloud.

**USE THESE LETTERS**

i  a  n  w  b  e

do_n          c_n

w_           o_e

_ut          _s

# UNIT 3

 Trace each word, then write it twice more in the space provided.

> me

> big

> come

> blue

> red

> where

> was

> away

> here

> help

Write each of your spelling words in the clouds below.

Put the following words into their correct shape boxes.

**WORD BANK:**

help    me    away

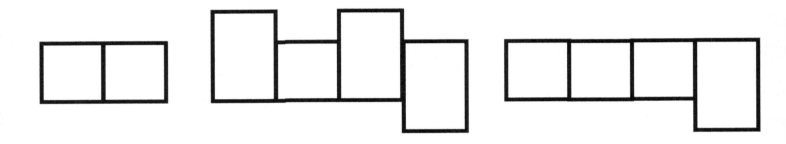

---

 Draw a line to connect the matching words.

| | |
|---|---|
| big | red |
| red | blue |
| come | come |
| blue | big |
| here | here |

 Circle the correct spelling in each row.

mee    me    mie    mi

come    cmoe    com    comm

ware    whare    wehre    where

was    wuz    waz    wass

awiy    away    awah    ayaw

holp    ehlp    help    halp

Use the words to the left to fill in the spaces and complete the story!

The sky is
_____.

It's full of _____,
fluffy clouds.

I watch them
float _____.

_____ do
they go?

# UNIT 4

 Trace each word, then write it twice more in the space provided.

> make

> many

> two

> jump

> play

> run

> find

> own

> funny

> he

Write each of your spelling words in the flowers below.

Put the following words into their correct shape boxes.

**WORD BANK:**

jump    two    find

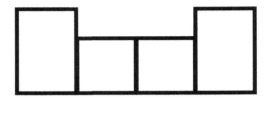

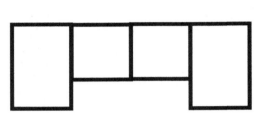

 Draw a line to connect the matching words.

| own | funny |
| funny | own |
| he | run |
| run | play |
| play | he |

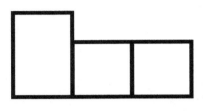 Circle the correct spelling in each row.

| fund | fied | fnid | find |
| two | too | twoo | tow |
| many | mony | manny | meny |
| mike | mack | make | mak |
| own | onw | oawn | ohn |
| run | ran | ron | runn |

1) Fill in the missing letter for each word.
2) Read each word aloud.

**USE THESE LETTERS**

k w p m u y

f_nny

_ _e

_Tay

o_n

_man

ma_e

# UNIT 5

 Trace each word, then write it twice more in the space provided.

> about

> fall

> in

> they

> but

> at

> with

> all

> there

> out

Write each of your spelling words in the leaves below.

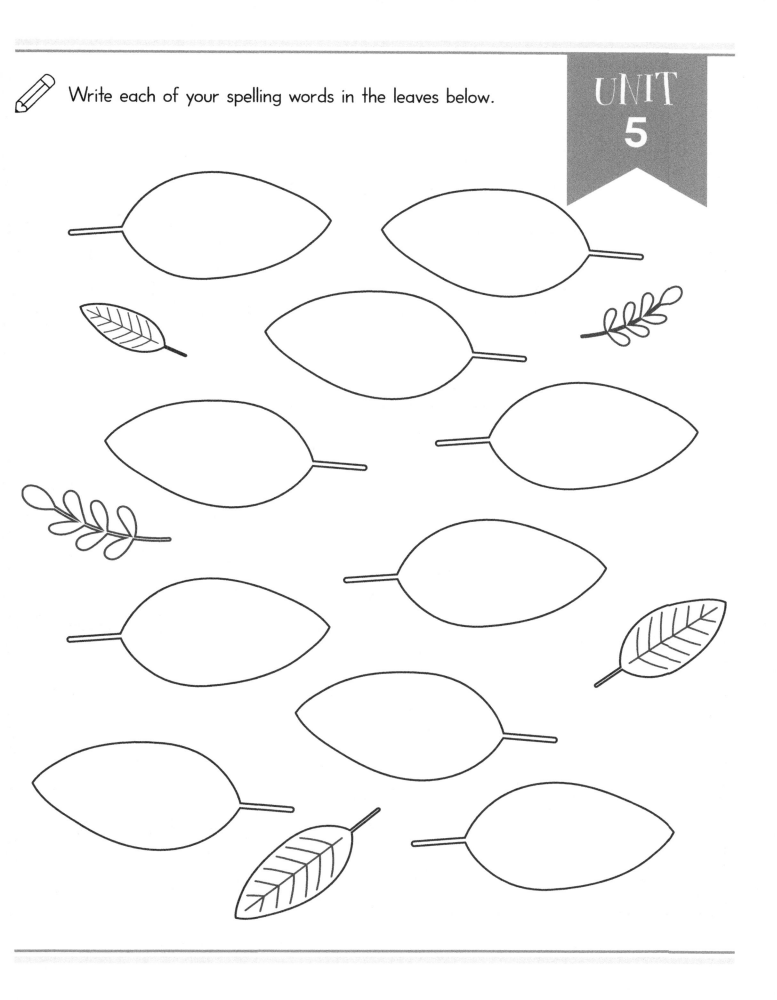

 Put the following words into their correct shape boxes.

**WORD BANK:**

about    fall    with

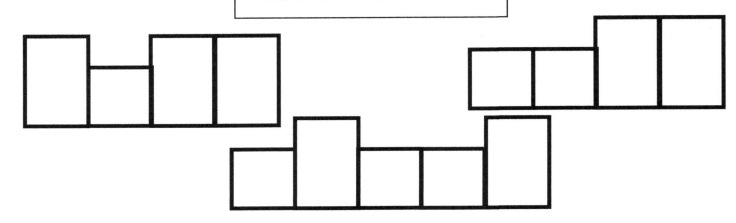

---

 Draw a line to connect the matching words.

out                they

there              out

but                at

at                 but

they               there

 Circle the correct spelling in each row.

al        all       awl       ahl

abut      abot      abuot     about

fall      fawl      fale      fal

they      thay      the       tha

ther      there     thare     tere

out       oght      uot       outt

1) Fill in the missing letter for each word.
2) Read each word aloud.

## USE THESE LETTERS

a  l  w  o  i  t

___hey

a___

ab___ut

f___ll

___ith

___n

# UNIT 6

 Trace each word, then write it twice more in the space provided.

- ➤ be
- ➤ have
- ➤ an
- ➤ tree
- ➤ did
- ➤ what
- ➤ so
- ➤ get
- ➤ word
- ➤ that

Write each of your spelling words in the tree below.

Put the following words into their correct shape boxes.

**WORD BANK:**

what    get    so

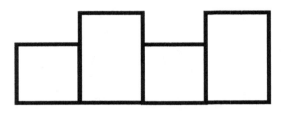

 Draw a line to connect the matching words.

| | |
|---|---|
| be | did |
| did | get |
| an | so |
| so | be |
| get | an |

Circle the correct spelling in each row.

whit    what    wat    watt

hav    have    huve    havv

thot    that    taht    tat

word    wurd    wodd    wrod

did    ddi    didd    ded

get    git    gett    gte

| | |
|---|---|
| an | That |
| tree | so |

 Use the words to the left to fill in the spaces and complete the story!

Is that
a _____?

_____
_____ is
a tree.

The tree is
_____ tall.

I see
_____
_____ apple!

# UNIT 7

 Trace each word, then write it twice more in the space provided.

> will

> cat

> yes

> went

> are

> now

> no

> ride

> into

> good

Write each of your spelling words in the pawprints below.

UNIT
7

Put the following words into their correct shape boxes.

**WORD BANK:**

yes    good    into

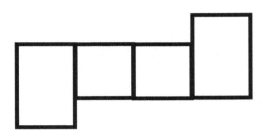

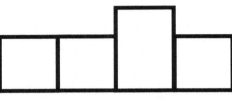

 Draw a line to connect the matching words.

| | |
|---|---|
| ride | yes |
| no | no |
| now | are |
| are | ride |
| yes | now |

 Circle the correct spelling in each row.

cat    cate    cta    catt

will    wil    whill    wlil

whent    went    wint    weat

ar    arr    orr    are

rhid    ried    ride    roid

good    gudd    goud    guud

1) Fill in the missing letter for each word.
2) Read each word aloud.

__at

goo__

in__

__es

r__de

__ent

# UNIT 8

 Trace each word, then write it twice more in the space provided.

- am
- want
- too
- pretty
- three
- saw
- well
- four
- yellow
- eat

Write each of your spelling words in the jellyfish below.

Put the following words into their correct shape boxes.

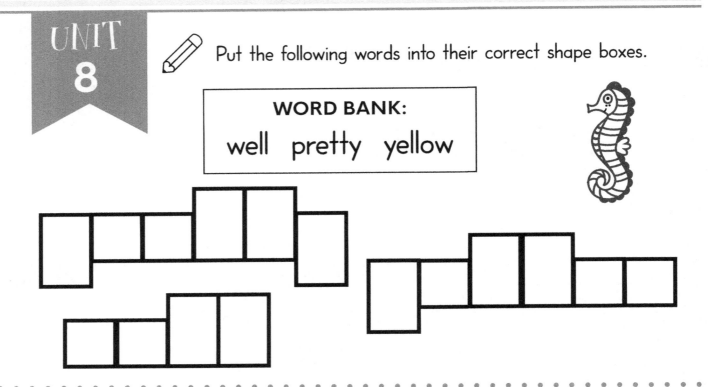

**WORD BANK:**

well   pretty   yellow

Draw a line to connect the matching words.

| | |
|---|---|
| am | three |
| want | am |
| too | saw |
| saw | too |
| three | want |

Circle the correct spelling in each row.

eet    eat    eta    eatt

yelow    yelloh    yellow    yelon

three    thre    threie    thrie

prety    pritty    pretty    preaty

well    weil    wele    whell

thrie    three    thre    thrie

three    too

pretty    four

 Use the words to the left to fill in the spaces and complete the story!

I see _____ jellyfish.

There are _____ fish also.

They are very _____ _____.

I think so, _____!

# UNIT 9

 Trace each word, then write it twice more in the space provided.

> new

> must

> black

> white

> soon

> our

> ate

> say

> under

> please

Write each of your spelling words in the crowns below.

UNIT
9

Put the following words into their correct shape boxes.

**WORD BANK:**

say    ate    our

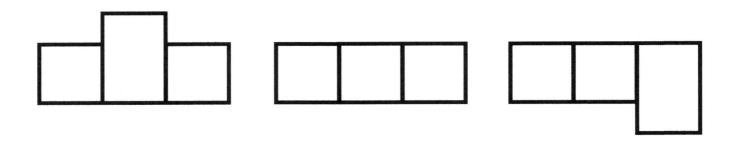

 Draw a line to connect the matching words.

| | |
|---|---|
| white | under |
| black | white |
| under | must |
| must | new |
| new | black |

 Circle the correct spelling in each row.

suun    sone    soon    sono

plese    plees    plaese    please

under    undre    onder    undr

seay    saay    say    sae

our    aur    uor    arr

ate    att    ete    aht

1) Fill in the missing letter for each word.
2) Read each word aloud.

b  y  d  t  p  a

Tack         Tease

whi e        un  er

Te           sa

# UNIT 10

> of

> his

> has

> him

> her

> some

> as

> then

> could

> when

Write each of your spelling words in the coconuts below.

UNIT
10

Put the following words into their correct shape boxes.

**WORD BANK:**

of    his    then

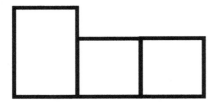  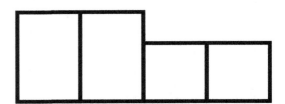

 Draw a line to connect the matching words.

| | |
|---|---|
| him | then |
| her | when |
| when | her |
| could | could |
| then | him |

Circle the correct spelling in each row.

has    haz    hase    hass

summ    some    sume    som

hur    her    herr    hir

then    tehn    tenn    hetn

cuold    could    coudl    colde

when    whin    whan    wehn

as      His

has    Some

 Use the words to the left to fill in the spaces and complete the story!

_____ The monkey
········· a coconut.

It's ····· big
_____
as his head!

_____
·········coconuts
are small.

_____
·········coconut
is big.

# UNIT 11

 Trace each word, then write it twice more in the space provided.

> were

> like

> ask

> who

> over

> just

> from

> any

> how

> know

Write each of your spelling words in the hearts below.

UNIT
11

# UNIT 11

 Put the following words into their correct shape boxes.

**WORD BANK:**

ask   just   from

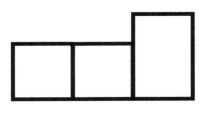

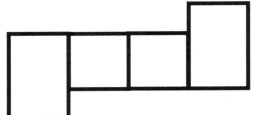  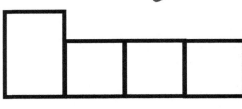

---

 Draw a line to connect the matching words.

| | |
|---|---|
| know | any |
| ask | were |
| who | who |
| any | know |
| were | ask |

 Circle the correct spelling in each row.

| | | | |
|---|---|---|---|
| like | liyke | lyke | lkie |
| just | juts | jist | jtus |
| frim | frum | from | frmo |
| ani | any | ayn | anny |
| hiow | hiw | haow | how |
| ovr | over | ovir | ovor |

1) Fill in the missing letter for each word.
2) Read each word aloud.

## USE THESE LETTERS

n  w  h  e  k  j

___ ust

ov ___ r

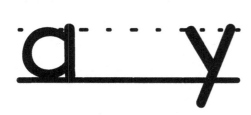

a ___ y

kno ___

___ ow

___ as

# UNIT 12

 Trace each word, then write it twice more in the space provided.

- put
- take
- every
- behind
- by
- after
- think
- let
- going
- walk

Write each of your spelling words in the turtles below.

UNIT
12

Fill in the following words into their correct shape boxes.

**WORD BANK:**

let    walk    put

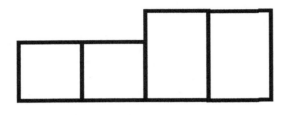 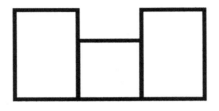 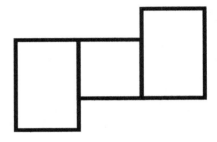

---

 Draw a line to connect the matching words.

| behind | by |
| by | let |
| let | walk |
| going | going |
| walk | behind |

Circle the correct spelling in each row.

pite    puit    put    putt

tike    take    tacke    tace

every    everi    evrey    everry

aftar    atfer    after    affer

theenk    think    tink    thinke

going    giong    goig    goong

behind     walk

going      think

 Use the words to the left to fill in the spaces and complete the story!

The turtle likes to _____ slow.

Where is he _____ _____?

The butterfly follows _____.

I _____ they are friends!

# UNIT 13

 Trace each word, then write it twice more in the space provided.

> again

> may

> stop

> fly

> round

> give

> once

> open

> had

> sun

Write each of your spelling words in the suns below.

Put the following words into their correct shape boxes.

**WORD BANK:**

may    stop    fly

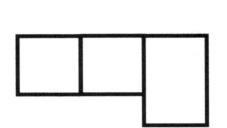

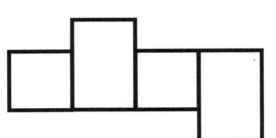

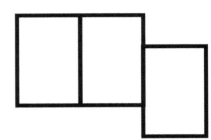

---

 Draw a line to connect the matching words.

give          had

once          may

open          once

had          open

may          give

 Circle the correct spelling in each row.

agan    again    agin    agian

rownd    ruond    round    rond

giv    give    gvie    igve

sun    sune    sunn    soun

open    opne    opon    opem

ince    once    onece    onche

1) Fill in the missing letter for each word.
2) Read each word aloud.

**USE THESE LETTERS**

f  n  d  a  o  g

roun___

___Ty

m___y

ope___

___nce

___ive

# UNIT 14

 Trace each word, then write it twice more in the space provided.

- this
- thank
- would
- very
- your
- their
- have
- five
- right
- green

Write each of your spelling words in the windows below.

Put the following words into their correct shape boxes.

**WORD BANK:**

very    your    have

---

 Draw a line to connect the matching words.

| | |
|---|---|
| this | your |
| would | this |
| your | would |
| five | right |
| right | five |

 Circle the correct spelling in each row.

| | | |
|---|---|---|
| thanke | tank | thank |
| wuold | would | woold |
| five | fife | fihve |
| rite | right | ritte |
| green | grien | grene |
| very | verry | veyr |

very          Would

This          five

 Use the words to the left to fill in the spaces and complete the story!

_____ you like to live in a castle?

_____ one is pretty!

It has _____ stars.

They are _____ bright!

# UNIT 15

> call

> sleep

> don't

> wash

> or

> before

> been

> off

> cold

> tell

Write each of your spelling words in the moons below.

UNIT
15

Put the following words into their correct shape boxes.

**WORD BANK:**
call   off   tell

 Draw a line to connect the matching words.

tell          or

off           off

been          tell

or            call

call          been

 Circle the correct spelling in each row.

slepe   sleip   sleepe   sleep

dont   don't   dntt   donte

wash   wassh   washe   washh

before   befor   befour   beefor

codl   colde   cold   cald

been   ben   bene   bien

1) Fill in the missing letter for each word.
2) Read each word aloud.

USE THESE LETTERS

e  o  h  b  s  r

‾leep          was

befo‾e          ‾een

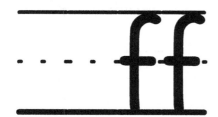

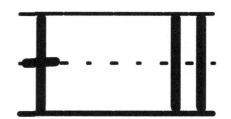

# UNIT 16

 Trace each word, then write it twice more in the space provided.

> work

> first

> does

> goes

> write

> always

> made

> gave

> us

> buy

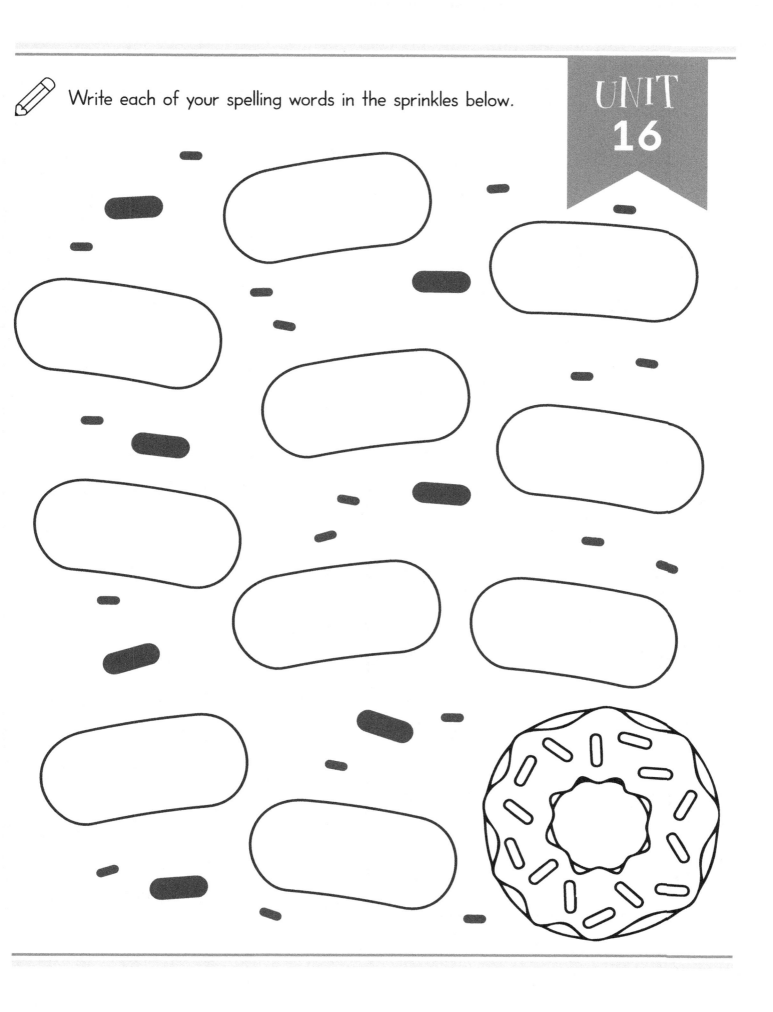

Write each of your spelling words in the sprinkles below.

UNIT
16

Put the following words into their correct shape boxes.

**WORD BANK:**

work    does    goes

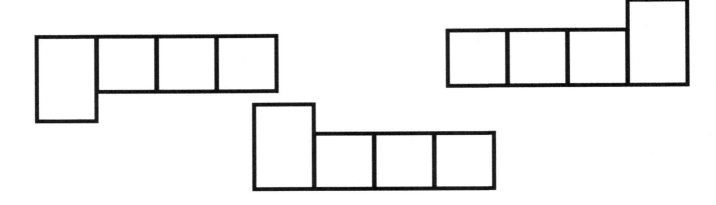

 Draw a line to connect the matching words.

first        goes

goes         us

made        gave

gave        made

us         first

 Circle the correct spelling in each row.

ritte    write    writte    writ

first    furst    fisrt    firsst

doez    does    deos    duz

mdea    made    maide    maed

bie    biuy    buy    buye

gave    gaeve    gaive    gaev

Does      buy

always      us

 Use the words to the left to fill in the spaces and complete the story!

I want to _____ a donut.

_____ it have sprinkles?

Sprinkles are _____ yummy!

I will buy one for _____.

Trace each word, then write it twice more in the space provided.

> those

> use

> fast

> pull

> both

> sit

> which

> read

> why

> found

Write each of your spelling words in the smoke clouds below.

Put the following words into their correct shape boxes.

**WORD BANK:**

pull   fast   both

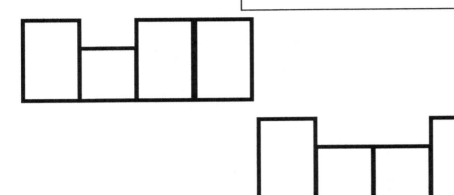

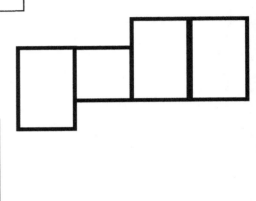

---

 Draw a line to connect the matching words.

| | |
|---|---|
| use | sit |
| fast | pull |
| pull | use |
| sit | fast |
| why | why |

 Circle the correct spelling in each row.

| | | |
|---|---|---|
| those | thows | thoss |
| which | wich | witche |
| reed | reade | read |
| fownd | found | fuond |
| pulle | pull | pul |
| use | uise | uss |

1) Fill in the missing letter for each word.
2) Read each word aloud.

## USE THESE LETTERS

y u f e i a

fo _ nd

wh _

wh _ ch

us _

re _ d

_ ast

# UNIT 18

 Trace each word, then write it twice more in the space provided.

- because
- best
- upon
- these
- sing
- wish
- many
- third
- long
- about

Write each of your spelling words in the shells below.

Put the following words into their correct shape boxes.

**WORD BANK:**

best    long    upon

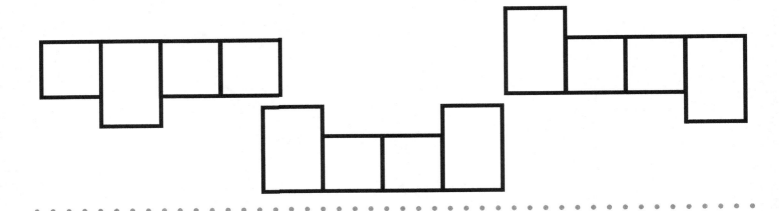

 Draw a line to connect the matching words.

about            wish

long             sing

third            about

wish             third

sing             long

 Circle the correct spelling in each row.

beecause    because    becuz

thees        thease     these

miny         manie      many

thirrd       third      tirhed

abuot        about      abought

best         bist       besst

about    best

sing    long

 Use the words to the left to fill in the spaces and complete the story!

What do you know _____ ........... mermaids?

I know they have _____ hair.

They can also _____ ........... well!

They like sparkling seashells _____ ........... :

# UNIT 19

> got

> six

> never

> seven

> eight

> today

> myself

> much

> keep

> try

Write each of your spelling words in the whales below.

UNIT
19

Put the following words into their correct shape boxes.

**WORD BANK:**

try    much    got

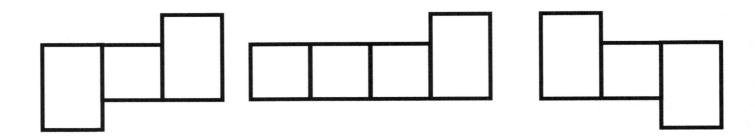

 Draw a line to connect the matching words.

keep                        six

try                        much

six                        seven

seven                        keep

much                        try

 Circle the correct spelling in each row.

eight        aight        eihgt

myself        msyelf        miself

today        tooday        todai

nevr        never        neverr

tri        try        trry

got        gaught        gott

1) Fill in the missing letter for each word.
2) Read each word aloud.

kee___   myse_f

___ever   ___uch

to___ay   si___

# UNIT 20

 Trace each word, then write it twice more in the space provided.

- start
- nine
- bring
- drink
- only
- better
- hold
- warm
- full
- done

Write each of your spelling words in the fishbowl below.

Put the following words into their correct shape boxes.

**WORD BANK:**

only    hold    done

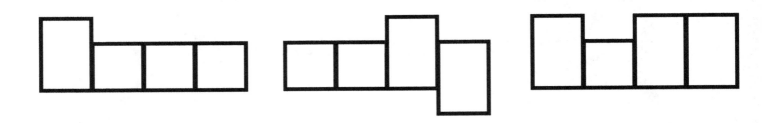

- - - - - - - - - - - - - - - - - - - - - - - - - - -

 Draw a line to connect the matching words.

| better | full |
|--------|------|
| warm   | warm |
| full   | only |
| nine   | better |
| only   | nine |

Circle the correct spelling in each row.

| start | starrt | statr |
|-------|--------|-------|
| brinng | bring | breeng |
| drink | drinc | drinke |
| beter | bettr | better |
| ful | full | fule |
| warm | warme | worme |

best          full

nine          only

 Use the words to the left to fill in the spaces and complete the story!

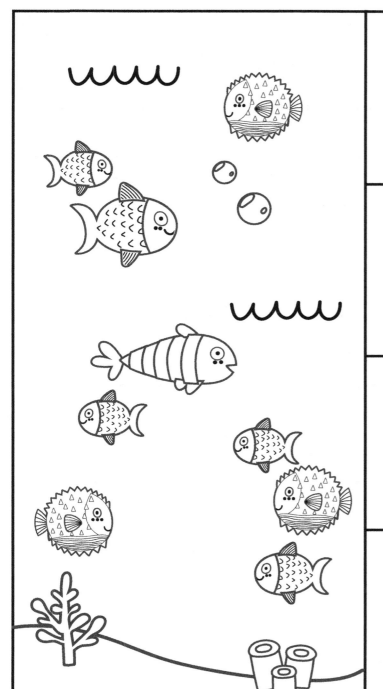

The tank is _____ _____ of fish!

I see _____ fish.

I like the yellow one_____ .

He is the _____ striped fish.

# UNIT 21

 Trace each word, then write it twice more in the space provided.

- light
- pick
- hurt
- cut
- kind
- fall
- carry
- small
- ten
- show

Write each of your spelling words in the giraffe's spots below.

Put the following words into their correct shape boxes.

**WORD BANK:**

fall   cut   hurt

   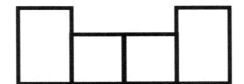   

---

 Draw a line to connect the matching words.

pick                ten

show                kind

small               pick

ten                 show

kind                small

Circle the correct spelling in each row.

| | | |
|---|---|---|
| smal | smalle | small |
| cary | carry | carie |
| light | lihgt | litge |
| fal | faal | fall |
| hirt | hurt | hurrt |
| show | shough | shouw |

1) Fill in the missing letter for each word.
2) Read each word aloud.

USE THESE LETTERS

s  g  w  t  i  y

carr

mall

p　ck

en

li　ht

sho

Trace each word, then write it twice more in the space provided.

> hot

> far

> draw

> clean

> grow

> together

> came

> laugh

> smile

> happy

Write each of your spelling words in the flowers below.

UNIT
22

Put the following words into their correct shape boxes.

**WORD BANK:**

far    clean    hot

 Draw a line to connect the matching words.

| laugh | happy |
| grow | grow |
| draw | laugh |
| hot | draw |
| happy | hot |

 Circle the correct spelling in each row.

| drwa | draw | draugh |
| laugh | luagh | lauhg |
| smill | smiel | smile |
| cleen | clean | claen |
| came | cime | cmae |
| happy | happi | hapy |

together     smile

happy        laugh

 Use the words to the left to fill in the spaces and complete the story!

The cats look
............................
_____ .

Yes, look at
them ............. _____ .

They are playing
· · · · · · · · · · · · · · · · · · · · ·
_____ .

They make
me ............. _____ .

Made in the USA
Middletown, DE
04 June 2021